BE THE CHANGE in your Community

VOLUNTEER

Megan Kopp

Crabtree Publishing Company
www.crabtreebooks.com

BE THE CHANGE!

Author
Megan Kopp

Publishing plan research and development
Reagan Miller

Editor
Anastasia Suen

Proofreader and indexer
Wendy Scavuzzo

Design
Samara Parent

Photo research
Tammy McGarr

**Production coordinator
and prepress technician**
Tammy McGarr

Print coordinator
Katherine Berti

Photographs
Alamy: Jeff Greenberg (front cover)
Dreamstime: p. 10, 11 (bottom), 12
Gotta Have Sole Foundation: p. 8
Thinkstock: title pg., p. 6, 18, 20, 21, 22 (bottom)
Wikimedia Commons: Public Domain p. 5

All other images by Shutterstock

Library and Archives Canada Cataloguing in Publication

Kopp, Megan author
        Be the change in your community / Megan Kopp.

 (Be the change)
Includes index.
Issued in print and electronic formats.
ISBN 978-0-7787-0624-3 (bound).--ISBN 978-0-7787-0636-6 (pbk.).--
ISBN 978-1-4271-7610-3 (pdf).--ISBN 978-1-4271-7606-6 (html)

        1. Communities--Juvenile literature. 2. Social participation--
Juvenile literature. I. Title.

HM756.K56 2014   j307   C2014-903840-2
                                          C2014-903841-0

Library of Congress Cataloging-in-Publication Data

Kopp, Megan.
  Be the change in your community / Megan Kopp.
       pages cm. -- (Be the change!)
  Includes index.
  ISBN 978-0-7787-0624-3 (reinforced library binding) -- ISBN 978-0-7787-0636-6 (pbk.)
  -- ISBN 978-1-4271-7610-3 (electronic pdf) -- ISBN 978-1-4271-7606-6 (electronic html)
  1. Community leadership--Juvenile literature. 2. Young volunteers in community
development--Juvenile literature. 3. Social action--Juvenile literature. I. Title.

  HN49.C6K665 2015
  303.3'4--dc23

                                          2014032610

Crabtree Publishing Company

www.crabtreebooks.com   1-800-387-7650

Printed in Canada/102014/EF20140925

**Published in Canada
Crabtree Publishing**
616 Welland Ave.
St. Catharines, Ontario
L2M 5V6

**Published in the United States
Crabtree Publishing**
PMB 59051
350 Fifth Avenue, 59th Floor
New York, New York 10118

**Published in the United Kingdom
Crabtree Publishing**
Maritime House
Basin Road North, Hove
BN41 1WR

**Published in Australia
Crabtree Publishing**
3 Charles Street
Coburg North
VIC 3058

Contents

Be the change!

Mahatma Ghandi was a great leader who lived a long time ago. He believed every person has the power to help others. He worked to make the world a better place. He did it in peaceful ways. It was not always easy. It took **courage** and strength.

Many people credit Gandhi with saying: "Be the change you want to see in the world."

MAKING CHANGE HAPPEN!

What do you think the words "be the change" mean?

Caring about people and the world is important. Gandi worked hard to make positive change. He believed anyone could do it. Even a small change can make a big difference. Changing our actions can change our world.

Gandhi still inspires people today.

Your community

A **community** is a place where people live, work, and play. You are a **citizen** of your community. A citizen is someone whose needs are met by the community. You can be the change to make your community a better place for all its members.

iDEA

If you like being outside, you can help out in a community garden.

Good to go

Help make your community the best it can be. This is one way to be a good citizen. Actions that help everyone support the **common good**. What if you build a playground in your own backyard? Only you can use it. But, what if you build a playground in a public place? Now everyone can enjoy it. The whole community is better off. There are many ways to act for the common good.

*You can create artwork to brighten up a **retirement** home in your community.*

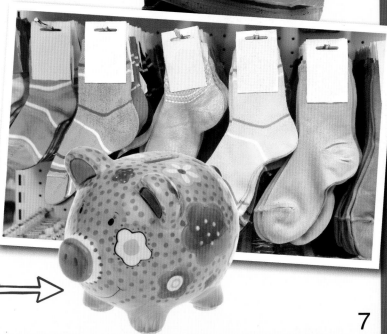

*You can buy socks or other kinds of clothing and **donate** them to a **homeless shelter**.*

7

One small person, one big change

There are many ways to make a positive change in your community. Nicholas Lowinger found a **cause** that he could jump on. He did it with shoes.

NAME:
Nicholas Lowinger

FROM: Cranston, Rhode Island

CAUSE: Providing shoes to homeless children

Nicholas cares!

Making change happen

Nicholas was five when he visited a homeless shelter for the first time. He wanted to show off his new shoes. His mom pointed out that some people in the shelter didn't have any shoes. Nicholas saw a cause he wanted to support. He started donating his gently used shoes. At age 11, Nicholas started the Gotta Have Sole Foundation. Nicholas and the foundation have provided new shoes to over 20,000 children living in homeless shelters in 35 states. He also started two new programs. One program gives shoes to veterans and their families. The other provides athletic shoes to children in need.

Growing change

Nicholas Lowinger found a way to change something. It was important to him. He started with a small idea that grew into a big cause. Change starts with the seed of an idea. Ideas can come from many places.

You might find ideas from:

- reading a book
- hearing something on the radio or TV
- seeing something with your own eyes

Do you like to bake? Make dog treats to sell to raise money for your local animal shelter.

*Do you like the outdoors? **Volunteer** to shovel a senior's walk in winter.*

What can you do?

You can use your own skills and interests to make your community a better place.

iDEA

Do you play a musical instrument? Visit a local retirement home and share your love of music.

Volunteer to mow a neighbor's lawn.

MAKING CHANGE HAPPEN!

What are your skills and interests? Make a list. Brainstorm ways to use these skills. How can you help your community?

Learning and planning

Look around your community and at the people and places in it. Do you see a problem that can be fixed? Or a way to make something better? Find a problem. Learn everything you can about it. Think about ways to solve the problem. Read books. **Research** on the Internet. Talk to people that can answer your questions. The action you take to solve the problem is your project.

MAKING CHANGE HAPPEN!

What problem do you want to help solve? What can you do?

Parks are fun places for everyone to play, but not if they are filled with garbage.

Sara wrote a list of questions for learning about her cause:

What is the problem I want to help solve? Too much trash in the park.

Who am I helping? Everyone in my community.

Why is this important? I like to play outdoors. So do my friends. We need to play in a clean, safe space.

What can I do? I can join a clean-up project.

Volunteer Sign Up

Sara
Darrin
Jeff
Amy
Lisa

To Do!

- Sign up for local park clean-up day.
- Meet at arranged time and place.
- Follow instructions.
- Wear gloves and sturdy shoes.
- Avoid wildlife.
- Take camera for "before" and "after" pictures.
- Have fun!

Time for action!

Now you know the change you want to make. Write an **action plan**. An action plan helps you know what steps to take to reach your goal. Goals can be measured. Meet the number and you meet your goal. Matt's goal for his book drive is to collect 300 books for his library.

MAKING CHANGE HAPPEN!

What is the goal for your action plan??

Ready to Read
January 27

Matt's book drive action plan

Matt wrote this action plan for his project.

Project name: **Ready to Read**

When: **National Literacy Day on January 27**

Goal: **To collect books for the Grades 1-3 library reading program**

Team members: **me, mom, dad, my sister, Auntie Sue, and my friend Charlie**

Where will you collect books? **From collection boxes in my school**

How long will it take you to collect?
I will collect books for one month

Set goal for how many books you want to collect:
300 books

Do it!

Now it is time to be the change! Matt worked hard to plan his book drive.

December 15 Get permission from the school principal for my project.

January 3-4 Collect and label cardboard boxes.

January 5 Get mom to drive me to school with boxes.

January 5 Put boxes in classrooms.

January 5 to January 27 Check boxes and empty daily.

January 5 to January 27 Store books on the shelves in my garage.

January 27 Load books into mom and dad's car. Drop books off at library.

Don't give up

Change takes time. Be patient. Remember why the change is important to you. One small change can make a big difference. Even if Matt does not collect 300 books, every book makes a difference!

MAKING CHANGE HAPPEN!

Who will you talk to about your project? Who can help you?

Share it!

You can make a presentation on the change you made for your local community.

Let others know what you have done. Share what you have learned with your friends and classmates at school. Spread the word to your family, neighbors, and local government. Invite others to join in. Keep the project going.

Here are some ways to share your project:

- You can share your photos of the change.
- You can draw pictures, write stories, and make presentations.
- Share how much money you raised, how many performances you made, or how many books you collected.
- Share your success and your story.

Matt made a list of ways to share information about his cause:

- Ask the principal if I can speak about it to the school at the next assembly
- Make a poster with pictures to hang up in the reading program room at the library
- Get my parents to help me write about the book drive for my favorite book blog
- With my parent's permission, talk to the local newspaper

Sharing news about your change can inspire others. Be the change!

You can write about your book drive on your favorite book blog.

Local Library
RECEIVES 300 BOOKS FROM BOOK DRIVE

You can share your story with the local newspaper.

Think about it!

You did it! You made a change. Now take a moment and think about what you have done. This is important. It helps you realize the **value** of your efforts.

Ask yourself:

- Who did I help?
- How did helping make me feel?
- What did I learn that I did not know before?
- What new questions or ideas do I have?
- Is there anything I would do differently the next time?

You did it!

Car Wash

Keep being the change. Ask yourself: what are other ways to be the change? Every day you can help make your community a happier and better place to live.

There are endless ideas for raising money to make change happen!

Keep your community clean and help the environment by picking up litter.

MAKING CHANGE HAPPEN!

How will you continue to be the change in your community? Will you make your event happen each year? Will you get more people to help?

Helping others helps you

You get what you give. It's true! When you help others, you get something back. It might be as simple as a good feeling. Or you might have learned something new.

Helping others helps you. It gives you the chance to:

- try new things
- make new friends
- build up belief in yourself
- feel needed and important
- see more of your community
- inspire others to make a change
- know that you can do anything you set your mind to!

Volunteer at your local library.

Collect canned goods for a food drive.

Learning more

Websites

www.ladybugfoundation.ca The Ladybug Foundation raises money to help with homelessness projects in Canada.

www.kidsareheroes.org Helping kids grow from young volunteers to caring leaders in their communities.

kidsmakeachange.com To get kids more involved in giving.

www.gottahavesole.org/ghs Nicholas Lowinger's Gotta Have Sole Foundation gives shoes to homeless people.

Volunteer organizations

www.freethechildren.com An international charity and educational partner, working to empower and enable youth to be agents of change.

www.habitat.org/youthprograms Habitat's youth programs for ages 5 to 25 involve them as leaders in the work of Habitat for Humanity to eliminate poverty housing.

www.lrwf.org/home.html Little Red Wagon Foundation to help homeless kids, those affected by a natural disaster, or facing family violence – among others.

Books

Friedman, Jenny, and Jolene Roehlkepartain. *Doing Good Together*. Free Spirit Publishing, 2010

Lewis, Barbara A. *The Kid's Guide to Service Projects*, 2nd Edition. Free Spirit Publishing, 2009

Sabin, Ellen. *The Giving Book: Open the Door to a Lifetime of Giving*. Watering Can, 2004

Taylor, Hannah. *Ruby's Hope*. Ladybug Foundation Education Program Inc., 2007

Williams, Karen Lynn & Khadra Mohammed. *Four Feet, Two Sandals*. Wm. B. Eerdmans Publishing Co., 2007

Woodson, Jacqueline. *Each Kindness*. Nancy Paulsen Books, 2012

Words to know

Note: Some **boldfaced** words are defined where they appear in the text.

action plan (AK-shuhn plan) noun A list of steps that must be taken to complete a task

cause (KAWZ) noun A reason for action; something to support

courage (KUR-ij) noun The ability to do something that scares you

donate (DOH-neyt) verb To give as a gift to a cause

homeless shelter (HOME-lis SHEL-ter) noun Place where people without a permanent home or place to sleep can stay

research (REE-surch) verb Collect information about a subject

retirement (ri-TIRE-ment) noun A time when a person stops working for good

value (VAL-yoo) noun The worth of something

veteran (VET-ur-uhn) noun A person who has served in the armed forces

volunteer (vah-luhn-TEER) verb To offer to do work without pay

A noun is a person, place, or thing. A verb is an action word that tells you what someone or something does.

Index